Purpose
Movement
Color

A Strategy for Effective Presentations

by Tom Mucciolo and Rich Mucciolo

Includes a Special Section
on Electronic Presentations!

Limitation of Liability

No warranties are made, express or implied, with regard to the contents of this work, its merchantability, or fitness for a particular purpose. The authors shall not be liable for direct, indirect, special, incidental or consequential damages arising out of the use of or inability to use the contents of this book.

Copyright

About this Book

This *second printing* of our book includes some minor changes but maintains the same, easy-to-read, comprehensive story about the *visual side* of the presentation process. The second part of the book discusses how to present more effectively and the last section deals with some issues specific to electronic presentations. In the visual design section, the images appear in color because a major component of our visual strategy involves the correct use of color.

We believe you can create a powerful visual impression, not from using images with special *effects*, but from images which specially *affect* your audience in some positive way! Our principles of **Purpose, Movement** and **Color** are defined and referenced, using full-color examples to explain our *strategy for effective presentations!*

About the Authors

Tom and Rich Mucciolo, founders and owners of MediaNet, Inc., have coordinated the design and production of more than 3,500 business presentations since the company's inception in 1985. They concentrate on every aspect of a presentation, from the message (scripting) to the media (visual design) to the mechanics (delivery). Working with a variety of resources, Tom and Rich have directed events from start to finish, giving them hands-on access to the full presentation process and the experience necessary to discuss the unique presentation strategy covered in this book.

DEDICATED TO

THOSE WHO PRESENT

AND THOSE WHO HAVE TO WATCH

◆◆◆◆

Preface

Congratulate yourself. You're among the select few. The top ten percent! That's right! Only 9% of readers actually examine the preface of a book. Go ahead, celebrate. You deserve it!

We laugh at so many things, especially statistics. But in many cases, statistics can be quite helpful. For example, some studies suggest that 55% of everything you say is judged from what you *look like* when you speak; another 38% is conveyed by how you actually *deliver* the information; and, only 7% is from the words you say. While the percentages may be argued, the point is that the majority of the message rests with the messenger. It's not that content is unimportant. On the contrary! Content is very important. It just needs to be clear and concise to be effective. The nature of the communication process is more visual than verbal.

Since the beginning of our business careers most of us have been approaching the communication process *backwards*. Think about it! Typical business procedure starts with a letter, followed by a phone call, followed by a visit. Check the communication process: *Verbal, to vocal, to visual*. Written, then spoken, then seen. We write, we talk, and then we finally meet.

Now look at nature, the way we experience life, beginning with childhood. We **see** things - *first*. Then we learn to speak, and finally we learn to write. *Visual, to vocal, to verbal*. Seen, then spoken, then written. That is the *natural* pattern we expect. In fact, the world is composed of a growing number of *visual creatures*. These are the people who get most of their information from a visual source called television. Since television offers eye contact and action, there is a growing need for *visual presenters* — those who offer direct eye contact and build action into the message.

Business presentations that ignore this pattern are less effective. It's that simple! The event must be highly VISUAL, steadily VOCAL, and minimally VERBAL to be effective. A successful presentation must be approached in a manner *directly opposite* of the typical business process. It's only *natural*.

The *natural process of human behavior* is what MediaNet has based its efforts since 1985. We began to research this process by examining the success (and failure) of our own presentations. We had so many questions. Why did some events succeed? What made the presentation work? Was it the actual information? The presenter? The visuals? The audience? The timing of the coffee break? The coffee itself? It seemed that too many variables needed to be controlled for an effective analysis to be done. There seemed to be no real way to build a formula for presentation success other than by trial and error. Or was there?

We tracked the performance results of over 1,500 independent events over a 3 to 4 year period in the hope of finding information we couldn't uncover in any current research study. The results of our efforts were surprisingly simple. We noticed that nearly every successful presentation shared *three elements* which changed or affected the audience in some physical or emotional way.

The elements involved the attention to **purpose**, the control of eye **movement** and the incorporation of **color**. By changing the way the audience *thinks*, the way the audience *sees*, and the way the audience *feels*, the presentation taps into the *natural process of human behavior*. That's the secret! Presentations that *change* or affect the human elements of the audience are more effective. This change is not only as a result of quality content, but from the planned delivery of the information, as well.

The message, the media and the mechanics must work in tandem to produce a memorable event. The goal is to heighten the interest of the group in some positive manner so that the next step can be taken. An effective presentation stimulates rather than formulates. The event involves rather than evolves. The audience is left wondering rather than *wandering*!

Our principles are based on the human response to information and our process is simple: **Purpose**, **Movement** and **Color** are the ingredients for a successful business presentation. The combination of these elements is our *strategy for effective presentations*. Thanks for considering our approach. Oh yes, and thanks for being part of the select few - you know, the 9% who read the preface of a book!

Introduction

At MediaNet, we have been creating business presentations since 1985. We have been involved in the design, creation and delivery of almost 3,500 events using numerous forms of media such as 35mm slides, overhead transparencies, and electronic still-images.

If we've learned anything at all, it's the undeniable fact that, for most people, presenting before a group can be a terrifying ordeal. To compensate for this fear, presenters will invariably try to HIDE behind their data. By this we mean that they will cram as much information as possible on their presentation media hoping the audience will concentrate on the data and not on them. The sad truth is that the audience won't concentrate on either one. They will quickly lose interest, become bored, and the presentation will fail.

In the following pages, we will not only **tell** you what it takes to create and deliver an *effective* presentation, but we will **show** you, as well. By following our principles of PURPOSE, MOVEMENT and COLOR you will learn how to correctly develop a goal for your presentation, how to hold and build the attention span of your audience through the effective use of eye movement, and how to affect the emotions of the audience by using color. Our principles are based on a number of years of continuing research and have proven effective time after time.

While most of the book concentrates on the visual design component of the presentation, we also discuss the mechanics of presenting. We'll explain ways to enhance your presentation delivery style using proper gestures, body movement and other basic techniques needed to improve your skills as a visual presenter.

This book will help you create clear, concise and more powerful presentations and help you deliver those events more effectively. When your presentation is visually effective it means you've made your point to your audience. This translates into CONFIDENCE in your presentation and confidence in yourself.

As we move toward a global economy and encounter diversified cultures, we find ourselves relying more and more on *visual* communications. Technology keeps allowing us to *see* one another more often in a variety of venues. So our presentations will be judged more from *how* we deliver the message than from simply the message itself. We MUST communicate *effectively* and *efficiently*.

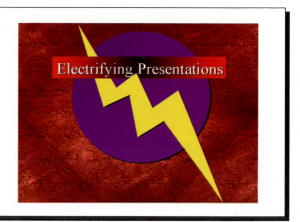

◆ The General Trend

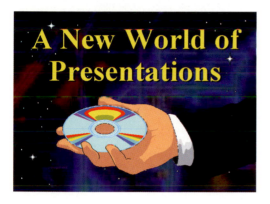

It's a *new world* of presentations! The information is complex, the competition high, the mindshare reduced, yet *success* is ALWAYS expected! In order for success to be realized, the visuals must be *effective*. Too often, however, we clutter the visuals with an abundance of content, leaving little time for the audience to stay attentive to the presenter.

EIGHT SECONDS! That's the average *attention span* on any visual. Oh, you can display a visual for an hour if you like, but the first 8 seconds are critical. That's when the audience must decide when to stop reading and when to start listening. The majority of the message is in the *delivery*, not in the data!

Since we can't read and listen at the same time, visuals need to be less cluttered to be more effective for the presenter. One sure way to increase effectiveness is to select the right presentation *media*.

Whether you use flip charts, overheads, slides or electronic images, the layout and design choices are *related* to the media.

For example, you would not use *builds* (elements revealed in stages) when *producing* overheads, but you might for slides or electronic images. The media choice shapes the message.

◆ Some Research

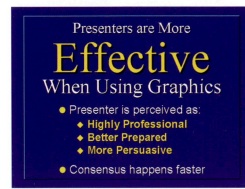

Studies have shown that visual effectiveness is achieved when the presenter uses *graphics*.

Geometric shapes, pictures, charts and drawings contribute to a more professional, better prepared and more persuasive event.

In fact, a *consensus* happens faster when the visuals are more clearly understood.

Studies also show that presentation graphics can reduce meeting time by as much as 28%.

Incorporating graphics into your visuals leaves less room for wordy descriptions and more room for concepts.

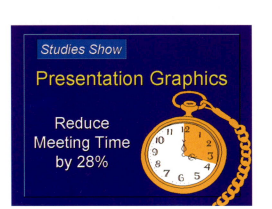

You want to get up, say what you have to say, and sit down.

Regardless of your approach to the visuals, each stage of development requires *attention to detail*. This takes time.

For example, if you do not allow sufficient *lead-time* for developing your story, the end result will suffer. Or, if you create images that are too *busy* (either verbally or graphically), the attention span per visual will be lower and the impact of the presentation will be that much less.

Planning the presentation should not be considered a chore - it simply needs to be *considered*.

After developing over 3,500 business presentations, we have been able to identify *three key elements* necessary for a truly <u>EFFECTIVE</u> event: ***Purpose, Movement*** *and* ***Color***.

By establishing a *central theme*, by paying close attention to *layout and design* elements, and by incorporating *color* into the presentation, your chances for a successful event dramatically increase.

When you can keep the attention of the audience on every visual without drifting (*purpose*); when you can control the manner in which the audience looks at or reads each image (*eye movement*); and, when you can directly affect the emotional response of the audience (*color*), you will have produced a very EFFECTIVE presentation.

As we examine each of these concepts, keep in mind that the more confident you are in the *visual* portion of the presentation, the more emphatically you deliver it! It's like attending a social gathering looking your best - you suddenly act that way!

◆ Goal-Oriented Approach

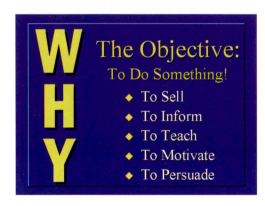

Perhaps the most critical mistake made in the development of effective visuals occurs at the very *beginning* of the planning process. More often than not, presenters fail to identify a single *purpose* for the event. Without a **central theme**, the story will undoubtedly drift and the presenter will lose focus.

Establishing a clearly defined purpose or *overall objective* is not only very important, it's **mandatory**!

Ask yourself "**WHY** am I doing this presentation?" The *why* behind the story is the **objective**. The objective must always be stated <u>actively</u>, as in: *to do something*.

To Sell, To Teach, and *To Motivate* are all examples of actively stating the objective for the event. By stating the objective, you begin to shape the story and slant the information in such a way that supports that objective. If the objective is *To Persuade*, then you will make sure that all information presented attempts to PERSUADE the audience in some manner.

When the purpose or objective is clearly stated, the amount of information you need to gather is dramatically reduced. The number of visuals required to support a *single* objective is less than the number required to satisfy *multiple* themes.

When you have <u>less</u> *excess* information displayed, the presentation becomes <u>more</u> effective. The last thing you want to do is waste a lot of time discussing things that are not *directly related* to your overall objective. Extensive details should be part of your handouts!

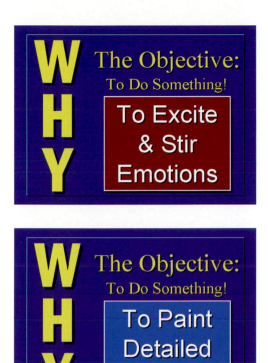

Sometimes the definition of the objective needs to be stronger. Simply stating the purpose as *To Sell* may not yield the results you may be expecting. When the objective is stated more emphatically, as in *To Excite and Stir Emotions*, the approach to the visuals automatically changes. The type of information gathered to support that kind of objective will be more *extreme* or more crucial than otherwise might have been used. Even the choice of colors for the visuals would relate to the more emphatic objective.

Consider the example *To Paint Detailed Pictures*. You can imagine the type of information needed for this objective. Each visual would contain precise elements that accurately depict the story so there would be *no question* in the minds of the audience as to how to interpret the data. Each visual would be carefully constructed to pinpoint a critical argument in the same way a painter captures a moment in time and artistically renders it.

Strong or powerful objectives, as in *To Force a Single Choice*, make it easier for the audience to agree to your point of view. The objective tends to make you gather information that is mostly one-sided and not subject to much interpretation or argument.

Make sure the objective supports a *call to action*; that is, your expectation of the audience. What should they do *immediately after* your presentation is over? Most presenters answer this question vaguely. But, the call to action should be *measurable* and clear or people will not act!

Keep in mind that the audience wants to know what is expected of them. You can't leave it to chance that people will understand what to do next. You must provide a direction for your audience to follow.

A strong objective demands a clear call to action.

◆ Remaining Focused

OBJECTIVE
Every Picture
Tells a Story

OBJECTIVE
Every Picture
Tells ✗ Story
^
the

Invariably, the shape of the entire presentation is affected by its original purpose. Those who ignore establishing a clear objective (and only one objective), risk success. If your presentation is not doing *something*, then it is obviously doing *nothing*, except maybe wasting time!

When taken one visual at a time, the objective makes it easier to construct a solid argument. Each visual should support the objective or it shouldn't be part of the presentation. It's that simple!

It's not that every picture tells **a** story, but that every picture tells **THE** story.

When visuals in a presentation do not relate directly to the objective they tend to require more explanation or more discussion. This happens in situations where the information on the visual is very cluttered or busy.

Chances are the presenter could have covered the material vocally rather than visually to avoid having the audience spend a great deal of time understanding the point.

However, by constantly focusing on the objective you will force each visual to make sense. If you take this approach, you will end up with a series of images which are *tightly woven* around a central theme.

You will require <u>fewer visuals</u> to establish your argument and make your point.

◆ Establishing Your Target

So how do you select an objective? Is it arbitrary? Is it based on any formula or strategy? You will know the objective based on what you plan to say at the very *END* of the presentation.

For example, if the last thing you plan to say is *"Thank you very much and I hope each of you will buy one of our products,"* then you are trying TO SELL. Each visual would then support the objective of SELLING something to the audience, whether it be a product, a concept or an idea.

The end controls the event in the same way a punch line controls a joke.

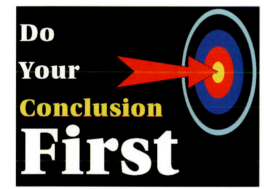

The key to establishing your objective is to design your **LAST VISUAL - FIRST!** This does not mean you will present the last visual at the beginning of the presentation; instead, it means you should do your conclusion first in order to set the pattern or direction for all of the visuals to be presented.

Your conclusion is the *verbal description* of your overall objective.

Think of your conclusion as a *dart board* and each of the visuals as a *dart*. Each image must be *directed at* the dart board in order to be effective. All visuals MUST point to the overall objective.

We have stated that when the purpose or objective of the presentation is clearly defined, the number of supporting visuals required will be fewer. This happens because a well constructed objective lets you *get to the point* quickly without displaying data that doesn't support the theme.

Less information means less distraction!

◆ Aspect Ratio

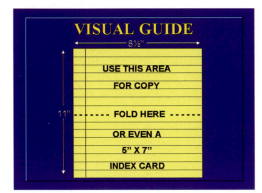

The design of the visuals using the information chosen to support the story needs to be presented in a *clearly readable* format, as well.

Most presenters belong to the *8½ by 11 crowd.* That is, those who use an *entire sheet* of paper to sketch out each visual.

The problem is that a visual in a presentation should not be designed on a full, 66-line typewritten sheet of paper. When projected, a visual needs to be clearly seen *from a distance.* This means the text must be large and the amount of data limited.

The suggestion for initial design is to *fold your page in half* before you design anything. This will force you into a *smaller work space* and help you avoid cluttering the image with extensive information that may not be readable for the audience. For greater flexibility, use 5" x 7" index cards to build your ideas. The advantage of index cards is that they allow you to organize your images (on a table, for example) so you can see your story at a glance.

Many software programs have automated features to enhance this process. *Outliners* that look like a notepad allow you to quickly arrange your thoughts by topic, while pre-building your visuals at the same time. You simply type your main ideas and supporting points into the outliner, which automatically translates your words into visuals.

Slide sorters offer thumbnail sketches of multiple visuals so you can rearrange images instantly and easily. At that point you would be able to see if images need to be added or deleted or if the order of certain visuals needs to be changed.

◆ Can They See?

A clearly defined purpose needs the support of clearly readable visuals. The ability for your audience to absorb information in a short period of time as each visual is displayed rests on the ability to see the screen. There are several ways to test if your images are going to be readable by the audience, *from a distance*.

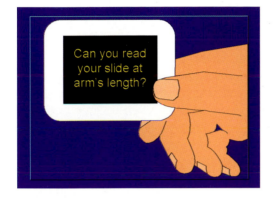

For **35mm slides**, hold the slide up to the light at arm's length. If you can read the text clearly, chances are the audience will be able to read the information when it is projected.

For **transparencies**, place the overhead on the floor and stand over it. If you have no problem reading the text, then the audience will not have a problem reading the visual when projected.

How the room is set up will also affect the visuals, especially regarding the lines of sight.

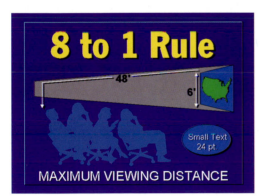

Use the **8 to 1 Rule** when considering the layout and design of the visuals. The rule states that eight times the height of the image is the maximum viewing distance for the audience to read small-sized text.

Small-sized text in terms of *point-size* would be about 24 points. This means that if you know your projected image will be 6 feet high, you would prefer audience members to sit no more than 50 feet from the screen, in order for them to read text of *at least* 24 points in size.

If you have a fixed-size screen, such as a TV or monitor, use the **One-Person per Two-Inch Rule** which states that for every two diagonal inches of the screen, one person can view comfortably. For example, a 25-inch monitor would be best viewed by no more than 12-13 people.

Most presenters tend to *increase* the amount of information on each visual in the hopes of clarifying major points. Nothing could be worse. Complex images cluttered with excess information should be avoided. Leave the details *off* the screen.

The key is to *hand out more than you say*. You should always hand out more material for review than you *verbally* cover during the presentation. You do not have to hand out exactly *what* you say, that is, a copy of each visual. After all, the *book* is very different from the *movie*!

In fact, handouts could be a combination of black/white graphics and explanatory text. Or, handouts may include your visuals along with an area for note-taking so the audience can create personal references for later review.

Sometimes handouts can be a distraction to a presenter if people are busy reading things rather than listening. You might wait until the end of the event to provide the handouts. Distribute the materials *in advance* only if the audience needs to reference your handouts *during* the presentation.

In addition, you should strive to *say more than you show*. The visuals are *speaker support* and only meant to **highlight** the script being verbalized.

Do not read the visuals to the audience unless you plan to use a *white bouncing ball* over the text to help people follow along!

Finally, you should *show it simply*.

No one will ever complain about a business presentation that is clear and easy to understand.

Simple visuals allow the audience to pay more attention to the message, and ultimately, to the presenter's point of view.

If you are able to control a physical element of the audience, you invariably command more attention per visual.

The parts of the body most used by the audience are the **eyes**. You need to find effective ways to appeal to the *eye movement* of the audience throughout your presentation.

For the purposes of this book we use the word EYE to mean *both eyes*. Also, the word "eye" represents an actual *focal point*.

Think about it! Where does the eye travel when it sees the visual? Where does a person look first? Where does a person look next?

◆ The Eye Needs Help

The visual on the left is a simple text image. The eye reads the title and then quickly scans the numbers in a downward fashion, treating the information as two separate columns. At about the third line (12:00), the eye *realizes* that the information should be read from left to right instead of up and down. This causes a loss in attention span in just figuring out how to read the information. What can be done?

Text doesn't guide the eye. *Geometric shapes* guide the eye! In the next visual, the eye is *trained* almost instantly to read left to right due to the incorporation of a simple geometric shape in the background of the image. Shapes are universal and know no boundary of language or culture. A square is a square everywhere in the world, but languages change across cultures.

The opportunity to assist the eye with graphic elements allows the visual to be understood more easily. This control of eye movement also allows more time for the audience to pay attention to the *content* within the visual.

◆ Creating an Anchor

Here's another example. The "Before" visual has no direction established. The eye will scan the heading, then the *30%* in the first bullet, then the syllable *trate* of the word *Penetrate*, and then the word *Cities* in the last bullet. This diagonal reading pattern is typical of the haphazard way we scan a visual. There is *no set path* for the continuous direction of eye movement.

The "After" visual uses a graphic symbol as an **anchor** for the eye. The jet trails of the airplane and the repeated airplane icons force the eye in a direct left-to-right pattern, on the first line and then down to the beginning part of the next line, on a line-by-line basis. using each icon as an anchor point. The eye has been given a direction - a clear roadmap to understanding the image more quickly.

◆ Geometric Shapes for Guidance

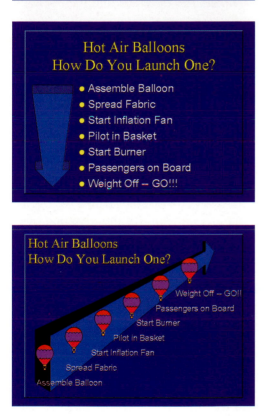

Sometimes you can affect change in the audience by adjusting the eye movement from the *expected* to the *unexpected*.

In the text image to the left, the list of items covers the basic steps necessary for launching hot air balloons.

The next image is the same but includes an *arrow* to show how the eye moves when it reads the list.

While the arrow is only there to demonstrate the point, consider it as a possible element for eye control.

Since the eye examines any geometric shape in its *entirety* in order to determine what it is and how big it is, we can incorporate an arrow into the visual and completely change the manner in which the audience *expects* to read the information.

In the next example, the eye moves from the question mark in the heading to the tip of the arrowhead.

Once the eye sees the *beginning* of the geometric shape (the arrow) it must search for the *end* of the shape in order to complete the image in the mind. The eye will travel to the end of the arrow at the bottom left corner of the visual and immediately continue scanning the image by reading the *first available* text element ("Assemble Balloon").

The eye automatically accepts the reading pattern from bottom to top, although this is not the *expected* method when reading a series of items.

The eye is graphically manipulated along the shape of the arrow, in an upward direction similar to launching a hot air balloon.

When the eye is treated to the *unexpected*, the attention span for the visual increases. The audience suddenly pays more attention at that moment simply because the eye movement pattern has been changed or altered in some manner.

The eye scans the most simple shapes, first, followed by the more complex shapes. Geometric shapes are easiest and text is more difficult. When you consider the shapes of letters and the translation of those letters into meaningful information you can understand why the eye scans text last and more slowly. This indicates that the design of the letters, the typefaces and fonts, affects the eye movement of the audience.

◆ Using Typefaces and Fonts

The problem with the visual to the left is that the contours of the letters themselves cause the eye to wander without any concern for the meaning of the words in the image.

Basically there are only two typefaces, *serif* (fancy) and *sans serif* (plain). Although names and shapes may vary, the general look of the letters falls into these groups.

Serif typefaces have embellishments or *curls* at the ends of the letters, such as the heading "NEW PRODUCTS", which has a typeface of *Times Roman*. In contrast, the word "Radios" in the first bullet is *Helvetica*, which is a sans serif or plain typeface.

The eye moves along the *contours* of each letter and will be more distracted if multiple contours or text shapes appear within the same visual. Fancy (serif) typefaces tend to *slow the eye* down over the contours of the letters. Yet, plain typefaces (sans serif) *speed the eye* along the less-contoured letters. We usually use a serif typeface for the *heading* of a chart and a sans serif typeface for the *body*.

We want the eye to slow down while reading the heading, which has less words, and speed up when reading the body of the chart, where there tends to be more text.

◆ Creating Inflection

MORE THAN SEVEN
CONSECUTIVE UPPER CASE
WORDS WILL FORCE
THE AUDIENCE TO
READ AGAIN

Letters also affect eye movement based on *capitalization*. Examine the visual on the left for a moment. Did you read it a *second* time? Phrases of text in ALL CAPS leave no room for *inflection*. When *all* words in a phrase have equal weight, you cannot place emphasis on specific text.

In addition, words in upper case are the same height. Without *ascenders* and *descenders* (as in the letters "h" and "g") the eye is given less comparisons between the letters. This reduces comprehension.

More than seven
consecutive UPPER CASE
words will force
the audience to
read again

By structuring text phrases similar to the way we read (upper case and lower case), you can use capitalization to place emphasis at the exact spot you wish to treat with more importance.

In this example, the verbal inflection is clear. the capitalized words stand out more prominently than the rest.

◆ Revealing Information with Builds

The Build Sequence

● Line ONE is revealed

The Build Sequence

● Line ONE is revealed (now dim)

● Line TWO is revealed

The Build Sequence

● Line ONE is revealed (now dim)

● Line TWO is revealed (now dim)

● Line THREE is revealed

This allows control of
EYE Movement

Eye movement can be affected by the amount of information the audience is allowed to see on a given visual. For example, the *build sequence* is a simple technique used to reveal elements of a visual in *stages* in order to maintain a steady focus for the audience.

As you can see in this series of visuals, the first line is revealed while the remaining information stays hidden. The presenter is able to concentrate on this element of the visual until the next item is needed.

When ready, the presenter reveals the next element, in this case the next bullet item in a list. We prefer using the *dim-down approach* for a more effective text build sequence.

Dimming the color of the prior element while revealing the next element allows the eye to focus on the brighter and most current item, while maintaining some visibility for what has already been covered by the presenter.

In addition, the audience has a *visual cue* as to which item the presenter is currently discussing during the sequence.

The build continues at the pace the presenter chooses, allowing direct manipulation of eye movement throughout the entire visual.

Of course, if you do use the build sequence, make sure you know the next bullet *prior* to revealing it or it may appear to the audience that you are discovering the information at the same time they are!

◆ Directing the Eye to Specific Areas

Perhaps the most obvious way to direct the eye to the important area of a visual is to *write emphatic headings*. In the example to the left, both charts contain the same data, but the second chart includes the emphatic heading: "*Fourth Quarter Soars!*" which directs the eye immediately to the fourth quarter as opposed to the other quarters.

When the heading is not emphatic, as in: "*Quarterly Sales*," the audience cannot react in unison to specific data since there are numerous areas on which to concentrate.

Don't waste the valuable space that exists in the heading. If something is important, try to emphasize it in the heading of the visual.

In the example to the left, the heading reads: "*Sales Swoon in June*" and the next image shows, with an arrow, how the eye will concentrate on the data for June.

As the visual is displayed, the audience is literally *prompted* by the heading to examine the data for June more closely than the other months.

The presenter is indicating a *preference* for this data-set since it probably lends support to the story being told. Emphatic headings not only direct eye movement - they manipulate the interpretation of the visual for the audience.

When you read the heading in the example to the left, you can *feel* the implied *negative impression* associated with the data.

Conversely, a simple change to the heading can yield quite different interpretive results.

In this example, the emphatic heading directs the eye to the *July data-set*. The next image shows, with an arrow, the area of eye concentration.

Moreover, the general impression you receive from the heading is now more *positive* than in the last example.

Used wisely, emphatic headings affect both the physical and emotional reactions of the audience.

Directing the eye using the *content of the visual*, specifically the heading, eliminates the need to touch the screen or use things to point toward the screen while presenting!

If you must point to specific areas of the visual, direct the eye from a *distance* rather than actually *touching* the screen. Touching the *screen* causes the visual to move or vibrate, while forcing you to penetrate the light source during front-view projection. The image should never appear on your body!

Avoid using a laser pointer or any pointing device in a presentation. The mixed metaphor of something moving (the dot) on top of something still (the image) is a distraction that leaves people concentrating on your manual dexterity rather than your eloquent delivery.

In addition, *your eyes* will be looking at the visual and your back may even be facing the audience if you are too busy referencing the screen.

If *you're* looking at the screen and the *audience* is looking at the screen, then *who* is presenting? External pointing devices are distractions to the eye and will reduce your effectiveness. Instead, consider using *graphic elements* as part of your visual design to help direct the eye.

◆ Using Arrows

Perhaps the simplest graphic element to use to control eye movement is the *arrow*. Although our last few examples used the arrow to *indicate* eye movement and concentration, there are numerous times where using arrows as *part of the visual* can greatly enhance the understanding of the information. The arrow is a perfect substitute for an external pointing device. Certain arrow *shapes* have implied meanings based on the *particular direction* the eye moves when it sees the arrow. The example on the left shows several meanings associated with arrows.

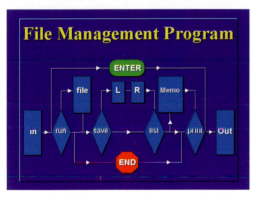

But, be careful with arrows! Eye movement can easily be distracted by using arrows which move in *several directions* as in the example to the left. The eye scans the visual elements and eventually wanders or gets lost. The colors, text sizes, inconsistent capitalization methods, and the variety of geometric shapes add to the confusion. The result is an ineffective visual.

The next example further supports the notion that too many arrows and line styles will distract the eye and reduce the effectiveness of the visual for both the audience and the presenter.

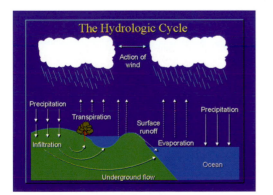

This visual also demonstrates what can happen when the eye is bombarded with multiple activities or thoughts. When you examine this image, perhaps your eye moves back and forth below the heading, and then down and up or to the side. The designer of this visual had a benefit that you don't have — the benefit of *time*.

Each element took time to create. But you are presented with all of the elements at once. You have no chance to see the designer's thought process — you only get to see the final result. Perhaps this complicated information can be served in smaller portions.

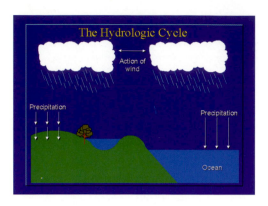

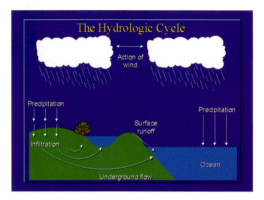

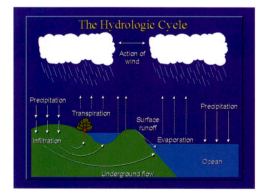

The image can be separated into several little stories or thoughts which, when combined, create the final impression. *Sections* of text, data, and graphics which contain complete thoughts are called *overlays*.

For example, maybe the *base image* is revealed showing the clouds, the land, the ocean and the down arrows associated with *precipitation*. Using our *8-second rule*, this allows the audience enough time to scan the information and then focus attention on the presenter.

The next visual, the first *overlay* (the second image in the sequence) adds a few more elements (infiltration, flow and runoff). The eye only needs to concentrate on the *new* elements added to the picture, since the other elements were interpreted in the prior image.

Finally, the last overlay (the third image in the sequence) adds the remaining elements (the up arrows indicating transpiration and evaporation). Once again, only the new data needs to be examined. With each piece of the "puzzle" added in stages, the audience gets a better chance of understanding what was originally a cluttered and complicated image.

So, if you think it will take the audience more than eight seconds to grasp the content of a particular visual, ask yourself if it would be more effective to reveal some of the elements in stages by using overlays.

There will be times when you may need to display complicated data. Using overlays will help you deal with the clutter by reducing the complexity into manageable segments for the audience. The less time they spend concentrating on your content, the more time they spend observing the delivery of your content.

◆ Establishing Depth

Time Distribution
Time spent by average employee

37% - Meetings
32% - Productive
14% - Telephone
10% - Non-productive
7% - Travel

National Statistics Council

Beyond height and width is an area of *depth* that should be considered for eye movement control. This *third dimension* allows you to direct the eye movement *toward* the visual. The next four images demonstrate the use of depth.

The first visual is a typical text chart which discusses how employees spend their time. It's clear, readable, and to the point.

When we decide to embellish our charts with other elements, such as clip art, we tend to shift the text to one side and incorporate the graphic on the other side.

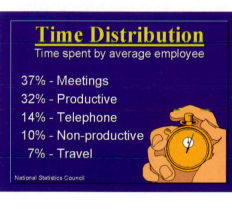

In the next chart, the hand with the stopwatch is placed in full view and supports the word "*Time*" in the heading. The graphic is now part of the chart. This is a two-dimensional approach.

However, there is an entire chart area to be used which occupies the area in the *background*.

Percentages can be displayed as parts of a pie chart, which is round. The stopwatch is round. Instead of making the graphic part of the chart, we can make the chart part of the graphic.

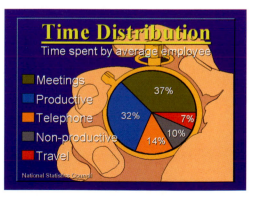

By changing the descriptive percentages into a data-driven pie chart and increasing the size of the graphic to fill most of the background, we can place the pie chart directly onto the face of the stopwatch. We then add the legends and other text to the foreground.

This creates the appearance of depth by using a series of *layers* to bring the eye *into* the visual. The use of the third dimension affects *change* in the eye movement pattern for the audience and increases the attention span for the visual.

Sometimes the background of a visual can be enhanced with a photograph to relate a more direct message to the audience. Instead of the stopwatch graphic used previously, the photo of people in a business meeting supports the idea that a lot of time is spent in meetings.

Too many of us neglect the valuable use of photography. Examine the product or service you offer. Do *people* use that product or service? If so, do you create visuals with images of people in the background?

Not every visual in a presentation has to include photos, but take a look at your script and ask yourself if a photo can add value to the concept being discussed at certain points. We are a growing group of *visual creatures* and we like pictures, especially pictures of people!

◆ Use Templates for Consistency

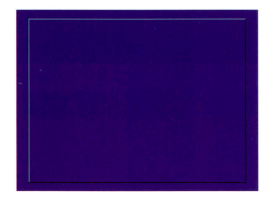

Regarding backgrounds and layered graphics, consider using *templates* or pre-designed layouts throughout the presentation. Certain software programs provide a variety of professionally designed layouts, coordinated with color and typestyles, which automate the visual creation process. This makes it even easier to build effective visuals.

At MediaNet, we produce a series of templates based on simple geometric themes similar to the one shown here. We realize the value that a simple visual look and feel offers. Templates help establish that consistency.

Builds, emphatic headings, geometric shapes, templates, and the creative use of *clip art* all contribute to the effective control of *eye movement*.

Perhaps the most significant event regarding presentations during the last few years has been the movement toward the use of color.

Since color has an effect on the *emotions* of the audience, correct color choices can have a tremendous impact on the success of the presentation. In fact, presentations delivered in black and white tend to *reflect* light and they are generally *less effective* for a number of reasons. These reasons will become more clear as we continue this discussion of color.

◆ Using Color and Symbols

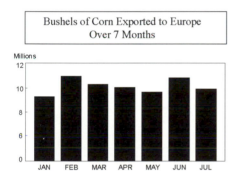

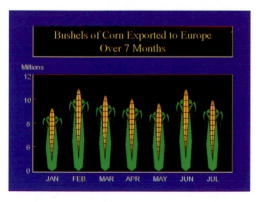

The visual to the left is typical of a black/white overhead transparency. Although the heading and the chart body have been sectioned-off using borders, the standard geometric shapes for the bars are represented by the solid-filled rectangles. The attention span for these visuals is usually very short.

By incorporating color and *representative* shapes, the attention span for the visual tends to increase. The representative shapes, in this case the *corn husks*, are actually graphic *symbols* from a library of pre-drawn renderings called **Clip Art**.

But, be careful with clip art! If the clip art remains in view for a while the audience may begin to examine the clip art for its details and the attention to the message will decline. It's not about the clip art, it's about the message. Sometimes the clip art can be a distraction instead of an attraction.

Apartment Starts
(Thousands of Units)

Apartment Starts
(Thousands of Units)

Quarterly Sales
Office Supply Division

In the example to the left, the X-axis and Y-axis are eliminated. The lack of color and representative shapes reduces the audience's attention span.

Most of the time, the heading may provide a hint as to the general category or type of clip art you may wish to choose for the given visual.

The trick is to create your chart in a normal manner, then find the appropriate symbol you wish to use to replace the standard shapes. In this case, we chose the apartment buildings from the clip art library to replace the bars in the bar chart.

First we position the symbol *on top of the first bar*, as a guide, and adjust the height and width of the symbol to the dimensions of the bar. We then delete the bar, leaving the symbol in its place. We do the same for the remaining bars until they are all replaced with symbols. Of course, if the clip art becomes distracting then the audience will begin to *play* with the visual. They may wonder if the people in the second building are really *taller* than the people in the first building!

In the next example, the subheading provides the clue as to the possibilities for the choice of graphics to replace the standard bars in the chart. *Office supplies* may include a number of items such as pencils, paper clips, staplers, and pads.

The important thing is to match the symbol as closely as possible to the geometric shape.

Adding color and the right symbol can make a difference in the amount of attention the audience gives to the visual.

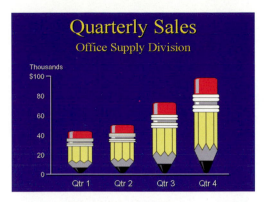

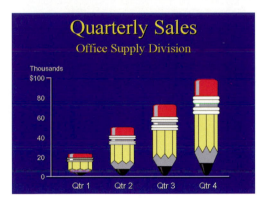

In this case, the pencils are both colorful and the proper shape to substitute for the vertically positioned bars. But be careful — clip art may not always be suitable in all situations.

What if the height of the first pencil was less than expected? The next example shows what can happen if the data element changes. Would you *give* someone a pencil this short?

Just because you have access to a clip art library doesn't mean you have to incorporate colorful symbols on every chart.

Use your own judgment when using symbols and graphics. If they are too colorful or too distracting from the information, then don't use them.

Also, be aware of the geometric shape you wish to replace. The bars in the previous examples were all vertical. The clip art shapes that were selected were also vertical. However, if the visual were a *horizontal* bar chart, for example, in the case of office supplies, a *stapler* may have been an effective choice, since a stapler looks more natural shown width-wise than standing upright.

If you find yourself *rotating* clip art to an unnatural position, you probably selected the wrong clip art.

If you intend on using photography or *natural images* as part of a visual, remember that photos usually contain hundreds of thousands of colors. If you attempt to overlay text or other elements on top of a photo with light and dark spots, the information may be obscured by the varying contrast within the photo. You may have to darken the contrast of the photo in order for the text to be more readable.

Readability is always the most important element to consider in every visual.

◆ Perception as a Reflex

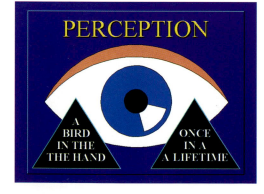

COLOR AFFECTS

- Mood
- Interest
- Motivation
- *Perception...*

While numerous studies have shown the beneficial results of using color in presentations, the most important reaction from color is more of a *reflex* than anything else. Whereas mood, interest, and motivation are subjective and harder to measure, the ability to affect **perception** is an underlying visual principle that color addresses.

Perception rhymes with deception and our reflexes sometimes out-pace our reactions, causing us to interpret information more quickly than imagined. For example, try this *audio perception test* on yourself. As fast as you can, spell the following three words *out loud* and then answer the question.

Spell the word **MOST**,
now spell **POST**, and now spell **HOST**.
What do you put into a toaster?

If you try this, you may answer with the word TOAST since it is a natural *reflex* of perception to spell the three **OST** words and then say TOAST instead of BREAD (the real answer to the question). Try the test on others to see if they react similarly.

The visual to the left is also a test in perception. If you read each of the phrases in the triangles *out loud*, you may find yourself reacting to another reflex of perception.

In both phrases there is a *duplicate* word. Reading the phrases backwards (an easy way to proofread documents) will let you spot the errors. But if you scanned the visual and didn't notice the duplicate words, you simply perceived the phrases using a common reflex action.

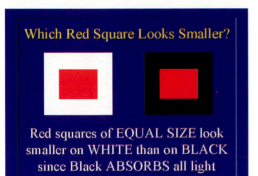

Which Red Square Looks Smaller?

Red squares of EQUAL SIZE look
smaller on WHITE than on BLACK
since Black ABSORBS all light

COLOR perception works much in the same way. This example harbors the essence of color effectiveness regarding business presentations.

BLACK ABSORBS ALL LIGHT.

This is the *major* reason why **black/white** overhead presentations are *less* effective. The data on these visuals *absorbs light* and pulls the eye into the visual; yet, the clear (white) background is *reflecting white light* into the audience. This is too distracting.

In a short while, the eye cannot handle the distraction. The eye tries to avoid the conflict and with it, avoids the *content* of the presentation. **Too much white light is a distraction**. Try staring at the fluorescent light in the office for a while or glancing at the sun for a few moments.

The white light problem with black/white presentations causes a distraction which may result in ineffectiveness.

This does NOT mean that black/white overhead presentations are useless. You just need to be aware of the distraction caused by the amount of white light and consider ways to reduce the impact of the problem.

This may mean designing the visuals more *conceptually* rather than more technically. Less words on each visual would let the audience scan the image faster and concentrate more on the presenter than on the screen.

Reducing the number of black/white visuals to be presented may be more effective, as well. To compensate for using fewer visuals, more detailed handouts could be given for later reference. There are many ways to limit the impact of white light distraction. Awareness of the problem is the first step.

◆ Red/Green Deficiency

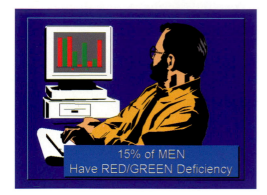

15% of MEN
Have RED/GREEN Deficiency

When incorporating color into presentations, be aware that certain color combinations may pose a problem for some people.

While studies have shown that nearly 15% of men have a red/green deficiency, MediaNet's research has shown that close to 22% of men have *some form* of this deficiency. Women do not suffer from this problem (in significant numbers) but they should be aware of this fact when selecting colors for visuals.

Those with the deficiency tend to see purple more as blue, or may mistake brown for green. The effect is not as noticeable with large areas of color as it is with *smaller areas*. For example, if a line chart has two or more lines using varying shades of green or red, some viewers may be unable to distinguish the lines. The result will be confusion and a loss of attention.

◆ Earth-to-Sky Color Theory

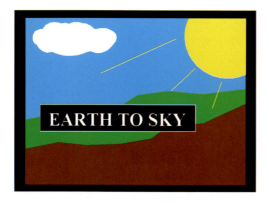

EARTH TO SKY

Regarding *related foreground* elements, the order in which colors are selected should follow the most *natural viewing pattern*.

Try to follow the EARTH-TO-SKY theory which calls for the arrangement of related foreground elements in a *darker-to-lighter* pattern from the bottom of the chart, upward.

We perceive color in the same way we view the earth to the sky. The earth is darker than the trees which are darker than the sky.

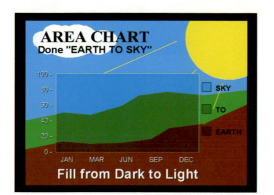

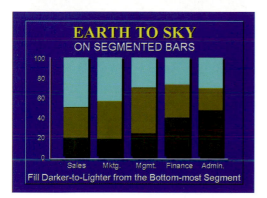

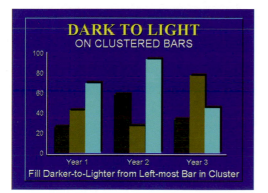

Related elements are most common in data-driven charts such as bar or area charts. On the left, the area chart demonstrates the Earth-to-Sky theory.

While you may select any three colors to distinguish the separate areas, the colors should be arranged darker to lighter as you look upward. The same would be true for other data-driven charts involving multiple elements.

The segmented *vertical* bar chart shows the darker-to-lighter pattern used effectively. If the top segment had been the darkest color, the chart would appear top-heavy.

The arrangement of colors, done naturally, allows the eye to scan the visual more quickly. Once the visual is scanned, the audience has more time to *listen* to the presenter's description of the information. Less time spent reading means more time spent listening.

If the order of the colors can make a difference, why not use it to your advantage?

The Earth-to-Sky theory can be applied to other data-driven charts, as well. When displaying clusters of bars, for example, choose a darker-to-lighter pattern starting from the *left-most* bar in each cluster.

Don't use the piano-key approach by putting the lightest color in between surrounding darker colors. When looking from left to right, the eye scans colors more easily when the arrangement is a dark-to-light pattern.

Remember, the earth-to-sky theory is for the related foreground elements in the visual, not the background color. Specifically, the theory is most useful in data-driven charts which utilize a series of related items distinguished by color.

◆ Emotions and Background Color

Large areas of color, specifically the *background color*, cause emotional response in the audience. The effect of specific backgrounds includes cultural reactions to what certain colors mean or represent. The psychology behind the color background goes beyond our general references into a deeper significance.

Keep in mind that society agrees on *associations* for colors based on appearances or cultural habits. Yet these associations are not universally accepted. For example, *green* is associated with *money* in the United States, but green is not the color of money all over world. So green can't really *mean* money. Color associations are tied to a deeper, more emotional reference that each color signifies. There's more to color than mere association or *attachment*.

Since we cannot rely on cultural associations regarding color, we must consider the emotional responses specific color backgrounds can generate when used properly.

It is the *background* color (not the foreground elements) that determines the emotional response from the audience. For example, where red may have the cultural attachment of *fear, danger,* or *stop,* the underlying emotional effect implies *desire, passion,* or *competition.*

All people, regardless of culture, share a similarity of emotions. Happiness, sadness, excitement, anxiety, desire, passion, etc. The ability to tap into these emotions using correct color choices can increase the effectiveness of the presentation. Conversely, incorrect color choices may lead to an emotional response from the audience that is different than expected.

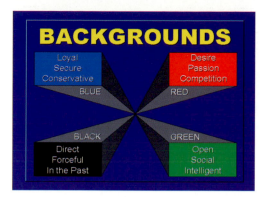

We might use *RED* backgrounds, for example, in presentations which seek to heighten the emotions of the audience, such as sales or marketing events. We lean toward darker shades of the color. In the case of red, we would select maroon or burgundy, rather than bright red.

BLUE backgrounds indicate a *conservative* approach to the information while maintaining credibility. When in doubt, choose dark blue or indigo backgrounds with yellow and white text. This combination is the easiest to read from any distance.

BLACK backgrounds are great for financial presentations mainly because black represents *what has already happened* or *what is in the past* that cannot be changed.

GREEN stimulates *interaction* from the audience. Backgrounds using a deep green or even a teal (blue/green) will help elicit opinions and are useful for training and education-oriented presentations.

Be careful with colors – too many will make the presentation look like a circus. This reduces effectiveness.

The use of too many foreground colors and poorly selected backgrounds will become a distraction for the eye and result in an ineffective presentation.

We have only touched briefly on background color choices. There is a complete section on Business Backgrounds which follows shortly.

◆ Using the Concepts

CASE STUDY

Given data, covering 5 months of
sales volume for 5 categories,
indicate that the 4th month
was the company's BEST.

CASE STUDY

Given data, covering 5 months of
sales volume for 5 categories,
indicate that the 4th month
was the company's BEST.

Sales Over 5 Months
(In Millions)

CATEGORY	Jan	Feb	Mar	Apr	May
Product	10.2	18.6	24.6	31.6	19.6
Services	6.5	11.4	16.6	24.7	20.4
Training	2.3	4.6	5.2	16.4	3.2
Rentals	4.2	6.3	8.4	16.2	5.7
Education	1.1	3.7	12.9	14.2	3.8
Totals	24.3	44.6	67.7	103.1	52.7

Let's see how much we have learned from our brief discussion of *Purpose, Movement* and *Color*.

Examine our **case study**.

Imagine we are given a spreadsheet of data which covers sales volume for five categories of the products and services our company offers.

In addition, we cannot change the chart into a data-driven type such as a pie, bar, or line, and we must present all the information on *one chart* (no builds or overlays).

From the statement in this case study, the *objective* or the *purpose* is clear - **indicate** that the **4th month** was the **BEST**.

It is important to remember this objective as we build this visual for our audience. In fact, we need to apply many of the principles of *Purpose, Movement* and *Color* to this case study.

The next visual represents five months of sales volume for the five categories. It is depicted similar to the way we might view the data in a spreadsheet.

The **problem** for most presenters *begins* here, mainly because most presenters tend to simply *stop* here. If this were to be our visual, we would have failed to attain our objective.

We need to make several changes in order to make the image more effective, and to allow the audience to grasp our objective within the first eight seconds the visual is displayed. But what more can be done?

We can start by *adding color*. We can vary the contrast in the foreground elements to highlight the *April* column. The *dim-down* approach on some of the numbers maintains their visibility but attaches less importance to those columns. The April column appears more emphatic due to the bright white text contrasted against the dark background.

In addition, the choice of *rounding* all the data to the nearest whole number adds more space between the columns, giving the chart a cleaner and simpler look. Removing the decimals keeps the audience from doing the math!

Yet, there's STILL more that can be done!

By incorporating a *graphic symbol* in the background and making the data part of the graphic, we can instantly satisfy the objective of indicating that the *4th month* was the BEST.

Even the heading can be made more *emphatic* to direct the eye to the most important part of the chart while suggesting the enthusiasm and excitement behind the information. The chart can be understood in just a *few seconds*, which is what makes it so effective.

Our *purpose* is clear, the *eye movement* of the audience has been directed, and we've incorporated an excellent use of *color* within the visual.

The next time you prepare a presentation, pay attention to the principles of **Purpose**, **Movement** and **Color** in order to be more *visually effective*!

◆ Business Backgrounds

The most effective presentations incorporate a **planned** use of color in the *background*.

Over the years, our studies have proven that the background color of the visual produces an emotional response from the audience.

After much research, we have developed a method for incorporating certain color backgrounds to achieve desired objectives and emotions throughout a presentation.

The following visuals indicate the interpretations or meanings commonly associated with various background colors and the recommendations we have for effective use of each particular color.

While there may be a number of different *cultural* interpretations of colors, the **physical effect** of the color is always the same.

For example, red is the *warmest* color in the spectrum and is seen that way despite what cultural associations we make, such as *negativity* or *loss* (e.g., "the company is *in the red*").

Let's examine the uses of specific background colors in presentations.

GRAY

- Neutrality
- Border between directions
- Un-committed and un-involved
- Concealment from other emotions
- Escape from anxiety and discontent

Gray represents a neutrality and lack of commitment.

Depending on the persuasiveness of your argument, the use of gray backgrounds may be a help or a hindrance. We tend to avoid using gray backgrounds when displaying any business information which is *critical* in establishing our objective.

However, in situations where the information is left for the audience to make a decision, the use of gray frees the presenter from predetermining the audience response to the issue.

For best readability, we recommend charcoal or dark gray. Anything brighter than medium gray will ultimately cause *glare* from the visual.

BLUE

- Complete calm
- Increased sensitivity
- Loyalty, security, contentment
- Tied to tradition & lasting values
- Reduces blood pressure & pulse-rate

Blue represents a conservative, secure, yet more vulnerable approach to information. Deep, dark blue is the color of midnight and, like the night, blue has a calming effect on the emotions.

The most readable color combinations are known to be dark blue backgrounds with yellow and white text in the foreground. We term these the *"when in doubt"* colors for situations where you wish to create an impression that appears conservative or traditional.

We tend to put critical information on blue backgrounds when we wish to develop a credibility issue with the audience that appears based on tested facts and figures rather than speculation. The blue takes the "hype" out of the information and seeks to elicit an emotion of trust and loyalty for the argument being presented.

GREEN

- Operation of the will
- Resistance to change
- Analytical, precise, accurate
- Opinionated and self-assertive
- Need to impress and exercise control

Green acts as a stimulus for interaction since it represents the *operation of the will*. Educators, trainers, or those interested in involving the audience in a *discussion* of the topic may benefit most from using green backgrounds.

In addition to learning environments, information requiring **feedback** such as management issues or policy decisions may become more visually effective when green is introduced in the background.

We recommend deep forest green or olive green, or perhaps a teal (blue/green) background in these situations. Avoid very bright green since foreground colors such as yellow or white will not contrast enough for the audience.

RED

- Impact of the will
- Impulse, desire, passion
- Vitality & intensity of experience
- Urge to achieve results & succeed
- Increases blood pressure & pulse-rate

Red is the *warmest* color of the spectrum. The tendency is for the eye to move toward red more quickly than other colors. This movement is most evident with foreground elements, such as a red slice in a pie chart.

When viewing the color red, there is an increase in the heart and pulse rate. For this reason, red-based backgrounds tend to be *stimulating* for the audience and can lead to a heightened sense of realism about the topic, even to the point of increasing enthusiasm.

We may choose red backgrounds for critical business information such as sales or marketing results or for any situations which strive to persuade or motivate the audience to *action*.

The *intensity* of the red you choose is important. We recommend the darker shades such as maroon or crimson as opposed to fire engine red or bright cherry red. It's better to *tone down* the intensity of the red and use a dark contrast for text readability.

◆ Adjusting Red for the Audience

Studies have shown that males and females exhibit preferences for different types of red. At early ages (about 5 or 6) males tend to develop a preference for *yellow-based reds*, such as the brownish-reds (rust, chestnut, or mahogany). Males also tend to build a preference for the more pure reds, such as crimson and brick-red.

At the same early age, females tend to develop a preference for *blue-based reds* (maroon, burgundy, or cranberry). Since these preferences exist in childhood and carry on through adulthood, we can use this information when choosing colors for particular audiences.

To further illustrate this point, let's say we intend to stimulate our audience to action or persuade them in some way and we employ red-based backgrounds in our visuals.

If the male/female ratio of the audience is predominantly female, for example, we may choose burgundy or perhaps maroon, both of which have some blue tones mixed with red to produce the color. On the other hand, if the audience is predominantly male, we might lean toward a crimson or mahogany background to appeal more to the group. Naturally there are hundreds of other variables in the presentation equation, but if a preference for a type of red may exist, why not play into it? The choice is always yours, of course.

◆ Adjusting Red for the Presenter

When red is used as a background color, the emotional effect can be quite stimulating and effective.

Over the years, we have tested numerous color backgrounds for many different presentations. We are most careful when using any type of red background. We have noticed that the stimulating effect of red adds a buoyancy or *vibrant* quality to the visual.

In fact, the *warmer* the background (the more toward *pure red*), the more vibrant the visual. On the other hand, colors like burgundy or wine (with more blue in them) tend to reduce the vibrant effect.

We use this to our advantage if we know the *presentation style* of the speaker. If the person is very animated, we tone down the intensity of the red by leaning toward the blue-based reds. This allows the visuals to *complement* the stimulating effect of an animated presenter. Conversely, a more stationary (less animated) presenter will be complemented by more vibrant visuals, so we would lean toward the pure reds in the backgrounds.

There are so many opportunities to utilize varying shades of a single color, like red, for selected presentations. Keep in mind that the original objective is the catalyst for the background color (red, blue, green, etc.).

The *emotional response* you seek from the audience dictates the particular shade or mixture of that color you actually use in the background of the visuals. Be aware of all your options when choosing colors.

YELLOW

- Bright, cheerful
- Stimulates and radiates
- Hope for future happiness
- Restless and seeking change
- Creates anxiety if left unchecked

So often associated with the future, **yellow** is both stimulating and attractive.

In fact, people who prefer the color yellow tend to *initiate* actions or ideas, but in many cases they don't always see those efforts to their conclusion. In other words, they may start a lot of new projects but never complete them.

Left unchecked, yellow creates *anxiety*, in the sense that it constantly represents a hope for something better *tomorrow*, yet when tomorrow arrives the hope for the *next* tomorrow takes over and so on, into an anxiety-producing sequence.

Although yellow represents something bright and cheerful and eternally optimistic, we **never use it** as a background color choice simply for the reasons of *contrast*.

Yellow is too bright as a background color. It will *reflect light* into the audience. The *glare* produced by a yellow background is too distracting. The result will be a presentation that is ineffective.

Yellow is best used for foreground elements, particularly headings, especially since all of our recommendations call for dark backgrounds.

VIOLET

- Mystical union
- Magical & enchanting
- Unimportant & unrealistic
- Irresponsible and immature
- Attempts to charm or delight others

Also called purple or magenta, **violet** is a color that represents something *magical* or *mystical*.

The mixture of red and blue which makes violet is precisely what causes it to take on a magical quality, simply because red and blue are so opposite to one another that for them to exist together is more *fantasy* than reality.

As a result, violet brings with its charm the attached notion of unimportance and immaturity, something childlike and unreal.

We avoid putting critical business information on a violet background for two reasons: First, the data may be interpreted or viewed as unimportant or unrealistic and, second, those who suffer from a *red/green deficiency* would see the background color as a *washed-out* shade of blue – a color that cannot be easily recognized, named or judged.

If someone can't *understand* the color, it carries *less importance* and the reaction becomes "less important backgrounds probably support less important information."

We use violet backgrounds for less critical information such as humor, special effects, or transitional visuals such as the typical "*coffee break*" image so often used to indicate the end of a main portion of the presentation.

Also, we may choose violet when the objective of the event is to *entertain* or *to amuse*. Since a big part of entertainment is the use of humor and more lighthearted information, violet backgrounds would work nicely for the desired emotional effect on the audience.

BROWN

- Reduced sense of vitality
- Passive, receptive, sensory
- Establishment of a foundation
- Increased need for physical ease
- Desire for family, a home, solid roots

Pure **brown** represents the search for something permanent or solid to rest upon. The *need* for brown is to satisfy the desire to build a solid foundation which currently doesn't exist.

Brown takes the vitality of red plus the analytical subjective quality of green, and creates an *uneasy* physical condition by *toning down* the sense of vitality that a red generates.

This reduced vibrancy puts brown into a more **passive** role as opposed to mahogany or chestnut, which are brownish-red but lean more toward the *active* role of red.

We do not use pure brown as a business background, especially for critical business information, because data on a brown background is interpreted as "not standing on solid ground," hence, less credible and somewhat unstable.

BLACK

- Negation of emotions
- Extinction & nothingness
- Surrender and relinquishment
- Powerful, strong, uncontrollable
- Stubborn protest against current state

Black is the *absence* of all light and the complete opposite of white, which is the *presence* of all light. It is this *contrast* that makes black such a **powerful** color (or should we say *non-color*?).

Since black *absorbs* all light, elements on a black background will appear closer to the eye than the background itself. An object reflecting more light appears closer to the eye than an object reflecting less light.

Black derives its power from reflecting absolutely **no light** and hence, shielding any emotional interpretation associated with a particular color. When the emotional response to a color is removed, the reaction is one of surrender or relinquishment, as in having "no other choice."

Information on a black background leaves the audience with "*no choice*" on how to react to the data. It exists, as is, and there is nothing the audience can do about it. In that regard, black is usually associated with things that have already occurred and will not change.

Hence, *financial results*, such as accounting data, may be best represented on a black background since the data cannot be changed – it has already happened.

◆ Grabbing Attention with Black

Black backgrounds also have a powerful effect if interspersed *sparingly* in one or two spots within a presentation.

For example, if you're using blue backgrounds throughout your story and you wish to make a key point with a particular visual, use a black background for that image. The black background will temporarily stop the current emotional flow, enough for the audience to sit up and take notice.

The visual is automatically interpreted as *more important* since it took **control** of the eye, interrupted the emotional flow, and left the audience with "no choice" as to how to react.

We still recommend you stay *consistent* with a **single** background color in a presentation. Yet, one exception to this is using one or two well-placed *black* backgrounds to achieve an emotional interruption that can be very effective.

◆ Using Black Effectively

When all the backgrounds are the same throughout the presentation, the entire event takes on the *characteristics* of the background color.

For example, we may produce a financial presentation using all black backgrounds. The interpretation by the audience will be that the information presented is accurate, thorough and not subject to change. We wish to leave the audience with *no doubt* as to what the information means or how it should be interpreted. The use of all black backgrounds, in this case, will achieve that result.

While we may recommend interspersing one or two black backgrounds in a presentation using color backgrounds, we do not recommend placing visuals with *color* backgrounds into a presentation of all black backgrounds.

We have found that the change in contrast from no emotion to some emotion only served to confuse the audience about the media itself, rather than allow the audience to focus more closely on a specific point in the story. In other words, a blue background in the midst of all black backgrounds appears out of place, rather than more effective.

◆ Changing Background Colors

Normally, you should use one, *consistent* background color throughout the presentation.

However, if you are using one particular background color, such as *red*, and you want to change, then at least remain in the *same color family* (such as crimson or scarlet) rather than immediately switching to a completely new color family such as blue or green. Switching to a new color family is difficult.

You may need a transition color, first. If you decide to switch color families (for example, from reds to greens, then to blues, and back to reds) you can try using charcoal or dark gray as the transition color.

For instance, presenting a marketing topic with blue backgrounds followed by a sales topic with red backgrounds and a management topic with green backgrounds may be best handled with an introductory visual, between each topic, set on a charcoal or dark gray background. This *neutralizes* the prior emotional effect and allows the next emotional effect to start from that point.

Even so, we do not recommend changing color families within the presentation unless there is an actual break for the audience (10 minutes or so) before the next subject (and new color) is revealed.

Without a break, if you wish to change background colors during a presentation, you'll need a *reason* that is obvious to the audience, such as a *shift in topic*, or *change of subject*, or even the introduction of a *new presenter*.

Keep in mind that consistency is not broken by using different *photos* as backgrounds for some or all of your visuals. Photographs can contain over 100,000 colors, so the emotional effect is not from the color but from the image or concept *suggested* by the photo.

Overall, the goal is to keep the presentation as *simple* and *consistent* as possible, without running the risk of distracting the audience with multiple background color changes. The changes in visual designs and backgrounds may become noticeable.

We have found that when an audience is *more aware* of colors, typefaces, layout and design elements, and clip art, they become *less aware* of the content or point of the story.

◆ Don't Show Technique

Too often we become concerned with the technical aspects of the presentation and we forget about the objective we originally intended to achieve.

Keep asking yourself a number of questions about the presentation you are preparing. Can you say something vocally instead of displaying the words visually? Can you eliminate certain visuals by providing detailed handouts for later reference or review? Can you offer the audience simple expressions of complex information in order to keep their attention?

You must try to make your point without overwhelming the audience with special effects, distracting colors, excessive typestyles, and other inconsistencies which reduce the effectiveness of the event.

The *medium* SHOULD NOT be the message!

The *message* should be the message!

It's that simple!

Visually Speaking

◆ The Mechanics of Presenting

One of the greatest fears is speaking in front of a group. There are hundreds of books and articles on the subject of public speaking, yet the fear continues to plague many who must, at one time or another, deliver information in front of other people.

While our early emphasis in this book has been on a strategy for effective visuals, we believe the *delivery* of the story makes a greater impact on the audience. Since the greatest percentage of communication is in the delivery, the actions of the presenter, from a physical and vocal standpoint, can add value to the visuals and make the entire event more effective.

The mechanics of presenting are based on both *form* and *function*. The form is an external view; the function, an internal one. On the outside, a presenter uses the body and the voice; on the inside, the mind and the heart. The simplest way to begin developing a delivery skill is to work on the external elements first. This approach is the easiest way to see visible improvement over time. What follows are the basic skills associated with the external mechanics of presenting.

◆ Stand and Deliver

What do you do when you're in front of the group? How do you tell your story? What movements do you make? What gestures do you use? How do your words flow when you speak? It all depends on the *relationships* you establish with:

- ◆ The Room
- ◆ The Audience
- ◆ Your Body
- ◆ Your Voice

The *theatrical elements* of your own presentation style can certainly make a difference in the interpretation of the visuals, based on how emphatically and how powerfully you deliver your story to the audience.

◆ The Room

Your relationship to the room begins with your body positioning. It is important that you understand the layout of the room, especially the size, distance from the group, and placement of the screen (visuals). That information may vary from place to place, so you may have to make certain adjustments to get the room situated comfortably for yourself and the audience.

What we are concerned with is your consistent behavior, regardless of the physical attributes of the room. There are a few *universal* concepts that you need to adhere to regarding your relationship to the room in order to maintain maximum effectiveness.

- ◆ Think Left is Right
- ◆ Build a Triangle
- ◆ Plan the Moves
- ◆ Play the Angles
- ◆ Avoid Upstaging

◆ Left is Right

You MUST stand on the left side of the room – that is, the left side from the audience point of view. Since we **READ** words, in English from *left to right*, the eye searches for an *anchored position* to begin reading. The eye is less distracted if it sees the presenter speaking from the left, then glances slightly to the right to anchor and read text (left to right) and then returns to view the speaker again. Match the anchor of the language!

If you stand on the opposite side of the room (the audience's right), the eye must travel *across* the visual in order to anchor and then read. Listening is delayed and effectiveness is reduced. If you have *no visuals* for the audience to view, you should still choose a "side" so the audience anchors you to a consistent area of the room.

◆ The Presenter's Triangle™

The easiest way to choreograph basic moves into your presentation is to *build a triangle* between the screen and the audience. The shape is really an imaginary area that we call the *Presenter's Triangle*.

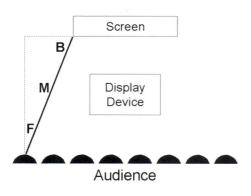

Screen

Display
Device

Audience

While standing at a fixed distance from the display equipment, draw an imaginary line from the eyes of the person sitting on your far right to the left edge of the screen. This is the long side of the triangle. It's like an *angled wall* that you cannot penetrate. From each end of the angled line, draw two lines meeting at a 90° angle to complete the shape. This illustration depicts the *Presenter's Triangle*. You now have a triangle around you. Simply play close to the angled wall using it as a boundary. If you step through the wall, people on your right will not be able to see the screen.

The good news is that there are only **three positions of the triangle** you need to be concerned with: the *front (F)*, closer to the audience; the *middle (M)*, where you should be most of the time; and the *back (B)*, closer to the screen. Treat the three positions of the triangle like *peg holes* or stopping points. Get to a peg hole and stop to deliver your information. In this way, you will not move around too much and, when you do move, you just get to a spot (peg hole) and stay there for a while.

Why must you move? The audience is composed of visual creatures who demand eye contact and action. The action is from the movement of the body. You need to change the position of your body every so often or people won't watch you. If your body is not adding value for the audience, then they have less reason to watch you present the information. They only need to listen. Listening gives them a chance to update their daily planners while you speak! Without movement you become a talking head. That's why the triangle exists — to create interest in your story from the language of your body. You need to move to the three areas within the triangle periodically, but not extensively.

Naturally, the illustration suggests you position yourself at a fixed distance from any display equipment. If you are using transparencies or seated at a keyboard, the triangle option is limited only to those times you take a position that does not block the view of anyone. That is why for overhead presentations, it is better to have someone else change the transparencies. For software presentations, use a co-pilot to operate the keyboard and the mouse while the pilot (presenter) delivers the information from within the triangle.

◆ Planning Movement

For the most part you will be in the middle of the triangle. But when the visuals are more *complex*, you will need to be closer to the screen so the audience has a shorter distance to look from you to your visual. When your images are less cluttered, you can navigate toward the front of the triangle and increase the distance between you and the screen. A simple visual requires less attention for the audience and allows them to concentrate more on you as you speak.

The lesson here is that *choreography drives content*. Although every visual doesn't need to be choreographed, decide which position of the triangle you prefer when making a key point and then look at the visual design supporting you to see if the level of complexity allows you to use the position of the triangle you prefer at that moment.

◆ On an Angle

You should be at a *45-degree angle* to the room. This establishes a *non-threatening stance* for the audience and opens your body to the screen when you need to gesture or move. This is a **rest position**.

To create the angle, point your shoulders to the *opposite* corner of the room. At the same time, make sure you can still see the people sitting on *your* far right. If you can't see them (even from the corner of your eye), then you may need to stand farther back in your triangle (to your right) or else you could be blocking part of the screen.

Of course, the closer you get to the display equipment (such as an overhead projector to change transparencies), the greater the chances for blocking the view of one or more audience members. This is one of the drawbacks to using media that you have to physically handle, such as overheads or flip charts.

After you establish a 45-degree angle to the room, you gain the opportunity to use the *power* of your LEFT SHOULDER. The theatrical move of *squaring your shoulders* to the back wall is a move of power and strength. It's a signal that the information being communicated is of *greater importance*. Each time you point your shoulders toward the back of the audience you move into the **power position**. But don't stay in that stance too long or the effectiveness of your words will *diminish*. The majority of your presentation should be from the rest position.

If you plan the use of your left shoulder, you can add impact to some of the more important points you make throughout your presentation. In fact, if you have some space between yourself and the front row, you can square your shoulders to the group and take one or two steps forward for even more impact.

◆ No Upstaging

Sometimes the audience is prevented from hearing your words simply because they can't see your face or your expressions. When a part of the body passes between the speaker's face and the audience, the result is called *upstaging*.

Turning your back to the audience is the most vivid example of upstaging. When you turn your back to the group, you eliminate eye contact and the chance to use any facial expressions. In addition, your voice is projected away from the audience and therefore less audible.

If you must turn your back to the audience, such as when writing on a flip chart or whiteboard, avoid speaking or increase the volume of your voice so the group can still hear what you are saying. In any case, when your back is to the audience, you're *least* effective.

Knowing that you must avoid turning your back to people, you should never walk into the audience. If you do, you will invariably turn your back to those you walk past, thereby eliminating them from seeing your expressions. Some people believe that by getting closer to a person in the audience the interaction is more personal. This is true with an audience of *one* but not true with a group. A presenter must treat each person in the group as an equal and must avoid favoring one person farther back at the expense of someone closer to the front. Keep remembering that the front of your body should always be visible to everyone.

Crossing the upper body with your right hand is another example of upstaging. If you must gesture to the screen, use your left hand rather than your right. If you use your right hand, it will pass between your upper body and the audience, causing a visual distraction that limits your effectiveness.

Use your *left foot* as a guide. For anything to the left of your left foot, use your left hand to gesture; anything to the right of your left foot, use your right hand to gesture. This will force you into a more open stance when presenting and allow you to add impact to your delivery style with correct gestures and movements.

◆ The Audience

Crowd pleasing is critical to the effective presenter. You must understand that the relationship between you and your audience is *mutually* beneficial. It is *two-way* communication. You just happen to be speaking and they just happen to be listening, but it all amounts to communication. In order to communicate your ideas effectively, you will need to do the following:

- ◆ Establish eye contact
- ◆ Reach out
- ◆ Phrase and pause
- ◆ Talk to individuals
- ◆ Get agreement
- ◆ Maintain control
- ◆ Smile

◆ Establish Eye Contact

Effective presenters LOOK AT PEOPLE. Making eye contact is critical to the communication process. The less time you spend looking at people, the less effective you will be!

If you find it difficult making direct eye contact with people in the audience, try this technique: Don't look *directly* into a person's eyes, look *between* the eyes. Look at the spot where the bridge of the nose meets the eyebrows and it will seem *as if* you are looking into the person's eyes. It works all the time. (Note: This doesn't seem to work with a *spouse!*).

In any case, the more eye contact you make with people, the more involved in the presentation they will feel. Talk to people, not to objects like the equipment, the screen or the exit sign.

◆ Reach Out

The *hand gesture* of the palm extended outward is a very *friendly* move. When you reach out to the audience, you appear as if you want the group involved in the event. The palm-up and arm-out position is generally pleasing to the eye and indicates a warmth of expression on the part of the presenter.

If someone asks a question, reach out to acknowledge that person. In fact, keep your arm outstretched with your palm up until the person *begins to speak* and then pull your hand back, almost as if catching the first syllable in your hand. It is best to use this technique for the FIRST question asked. From that point, the audience will feel more inclined to interact and ask additional questions.

When you reach out to the audience from time to time, you become more approachable and ultimately more effective.

◆ Phrase and Pause

Say a phrase and pause, then say a phrase and pause. By using this technique, you control the momentum or timing of the presentation. Each pause gives you a chance to make eye contact, or to breathe, or even to think.

Most people experience a general feeling that the time is moving too *slowly* as they present. The tendency is to speed up the delivery to compensate, but to the audience the delivery may appear rushed. Phrasing and pausing allows for smooth transitions and more consistent delivery. It actually eliminates the verbal fillers (such as *um, uh, er*) used to cover up thinking time.

◆ Talk to Individuals

If you *know* a person's name, use it when you reference that person. Think about how you would feel if you raised your hand to ask a question and the presenter knew your name but elected to identify you by your seat number instead.

If your presentation is to an audience you have never met before, it would be difficult to identify people by name, but you could reference individuals by asking them to stand or by requesting they identify themselves to the audience before they speak.

Each of these actions makes the audience more conscious of one another and more respectful of your ability to care enough to take the time to *individualize* people in the group.

◆ Get Agreement

If you nod your head to a person in the audience, chances are they will return the gesture and nod back to you. If you make the effort to get *agreement* then the points you make seem to make more sense.

Another way to get agreement is to use phrases such as *"Do you agree?"* or *"Am I correct?"* in your delivery. Visually or verbally getting agreement helps to justify the *purpose* of the event for the audience and keeps the attention from dropping.

When the audience physically responds to your gestures the way you intend for them to respond, your effectiveness increases. As more people in the group notice others agreeing with you, the overall impact of your story becomes more powerful.

◆ Maintain Control

Sometimes during a presentation you may get interrupted or distracted from your original purpose. This usually happens when the audience begins to ask questions. The response to one question may lead to another which is slightly off the subject. The response to the second question may prompt an even more remote discussion, and so on. This is a very easy way to lose control of your presentation if you're not careful.

It's best to simply announce at the beginning of your talk that you will take any questions *at the end*. This will give you the greatest control over the event since there will be little chance for interruptions.

If you decide on more interaction, control the *scope* of each response and be conscious of the number of questions you allow before continuing with the presentation. You may have to say *"I'll take one more question on this topic and then we'll continue"* or you may need to explain your requirement to complete the talk by saying *"We have a lot to cover, so I'd like to hold the remaining questions until the end."*

If you provide handouts or materials for your audience, you may lose a degree of control if the group decides to reference the information during your presentation. Avoid distributing information that you feel might be distracting until *after* the presentation has ended.

The more in control of the event you are, the more attentive the audience becomes. You will be perceived as *in control* and your effectiveness will increase as a result.

◆ SMILE

If you are not truly happy at what you are doing, it will show. If you aren't having a good time *giving* the presentation, what makes you think the audience is having a good time *watching* it?

Remember: You can't *get* an emotion unless you *give* that emotion, first. You can't get a smile unless you smile first. This doesn't mean telling jokes. It means that the audience looks for the *inside smile*, the energy!

The energy is in the enjoyment of your delivery. It is the *belief* in what you are saying and the *comfort* in the way you say it. The excitement you expect from the audience must be on your face all the time, because the reactions of the group are a *reflection* of you. Think about it. If you're not convinced, you won't be convincing and the audience will be less than convinced!

Unless the subject is tragic (disaster, war, crime, death), chances are that smiling during the presentation can only help. A presenter who smiles creates a comfortable feeling for the audience. People learn and retain more when they feel comfortable.

Do not equate smiling with a lack of seriousness. You can make very strong and serious points during a presentation if you've allowed the audience to see a softer side as well. The smile acts like a comparison or frame of reference for the group. They see you as a person with a calm disposition and a strength of character with the wisdom to show each side when necessary. They also see you as *approachable* which leads to interaction.

Without variety of emotion, there can be no impact. An effective presentation needs to have both drama and comic relief to establish emotional references for the audience. The more you smile during your presentation, the more serious you can get, if needed, to make a point. The audience ultimately expects to see some degree of entertainment with some evidence of enthusiasm. Enjoy your presentation and so will they!

◆ Your Body

Your body tells a story just as your visuals and your words do. But is your body telling the *same* story? The only way to effectively use hand and body gestures is to find a *starting point* from which to add movement. Your default position, without any gestures, should be:

- ◆ Hands to the side, always shown
- ◆ Elbows and knees unlocked
- ◆ Feet, shoulder-width apart
- ◆ Weight unevenly distributed

From this position all other movements can take place and look natural. The key is in **shifting your weight** to one side to appear more relaxed. A *relaxed stance* signifies authority, but a rigid stance shows subordination. A soldier stands at attention but a general looks relaxed.

◆ What About Your Hands?

Most presenters just don't know what to do with those things at the ends of their wrists. Some have a more difficult time using their hands in a presentation than others. Some seem to express themselves quite well with their hands, while others have a tendency to hide their hands; in their pockets, behind their backs, or folded in front of them.

If used properly, hands can orchestrate eye movement. Casual or emphatic gestures to the screen can create a visual inflection that helps the group recognize what is important.

For example, if you wanted to guide the eye with a hand gesture to the screen, you could simply lift your left arm and use your left hand to *motion slowly* in the general direction of the visual. This indicates that the image should be simply *glanced* at by the group but they should remain more focused on you. If you follow the gesture with your eyes and turn your head toward the screen, the audience will be more inclined to look at the visual, since you are looking at it, as well.

For more emphasis, you can raise your left arm and thrust your left hand *quickly* toward the screen, giving more importance to the visual.

Whether the moves are casual or emphatic, the key is to avoid making *half-hearted* gestures or the impact diminishes. You ultimately decide what gestures to use and when to use them. You cannot treat them lightly. Would you have a few visuals appear which were not bright enough to be seen? Would you casually whisper a few phrases that few could hear? You wouldn't make less of an effort with your visuals or your words, so don't use half-hearted moves when delivering the story.

◆ Keep Those Hands Apart

You should never hide your hands from the audience (behind your back or in your pockets). Avoid situations where your hands are clasped together in front of you. When your hands touch for an extended period (3 seconds or more), the audience tends to look at them and not at your face. The distraction reduces your effectiveness.

If you aren't making any gestures, then simply drop your hands to your sides. When you do gesture, keep your wrists above your elbows so everyone in the room can see the your hands. With your hands above your waist, simply avoid bringing them together.

◆ Pinkie Counting

One of the most common activities occurs when you hold out your left hand, palm up, and use your right index finger to count on the left pinkie, ring finger, and so on. This touching, or *tactile feedback* helps you remember a list of things, but the audience is distracted by the touching of the fingers from each hand. Simply use one hand, at your side, and allow just the thumb and index finger to touch once for each item you need to recall. The tactile feedback occurs, but goes unnoticed.

If you must count for the audience, raise your hand *above your head* and count for everyone to see. This will force you to limit those times you count *obsessively* and it will add impact to those times you need to count *emphatically*.

◆ Body Gestures

If you have room to move in your triangle, body gestures can create even more impact and increase your effectiveness. The key to all body actions is **to move with authority**. You lose effectiveness when your body *meanders* aimlessly while speaking. While you must have a reason to move when you are presenting, if you don't move with authority, the impression of your move is weak and the impact of your story is lost. Usually, you start meandering when you're less sure of your script or when you're not sure of exactly where to be next. This is why the *Presenter's Triangle* is so important. It gives you a defined area in which to plan moves with authority.

If you can't move from one physical space to another, you may only be able to shift your weight to create action. You can shift your weight from one leg to the other, but don't do that too frequently or it will appear as if you are rocking or swaying.

If you find yourself having to shift your weight more often, it is best to take a half-step *backward* rather than a half-step *sideways* to adjust your weight. When you move from side to side, like a pendulum, it is more distracting than if you move slightly toward or away from the audience. You can avoid rocking back and forth, by locking or tightening the upper muscle in the leg that supports the shifted weight.

When your weight is *unevenly distributed* and your feet are *shoulder-width* apart, you will appear to have a more relaxed stature. When your elbows and knees are unlocked, you have your best opportunity for movement. If your limbs are locked you lose energy. If your limbs are unlocked you unleash energy.

◆ Positions to Avoid

Be aware of what you do with your arms. For example, do not keep your arms locked at your sides as if your elbows were sewn to your rib cage. This forces you into the *gunfighter* position and limits the gestures you can make with your hands. To avoid this position, pretend that during your presentation you must touch the top of your head without bending down. This would be difficult with your elbows touching your sides.

Be careful about folding your arms in front of you. This *head waiter* position not only upstages you by putting your arms across your upper body, but it also indicates that you are hiding something from the group. With your hands locked under your arms, your gestures would be completely limited.

Do not clasp your hands together behind your back. This position, the *3rd base coach*, forces you to use your shoulders and your chin to create gestures. You'll end up throwing your chin or shoulder forward to acknowledge a question. The reaction from the audience member who receives that move will be negative.

When speaking from a lectern (also called a podium) or even from a table, make sure the *audience sees your hands* as much as possible. If you hide your hands, you're hiding something (at least that's how it is interpreted). When your hands are visible, they can be used effectively.

Avoid *conversationalizing* your gestures. This happens when you move your hands in the rhythm of your speech. It will appear as if you have a gesture for every syllable! You don't want to be a *hand talker*. The key to effective gestures is to keep them still once the initial action has been completed. The audience needs time to process each gesture and that is why your gestures need to *freeze* or stay still once your point is made. If you move your hands on every word, the audience will be distracted by the constant movement and they won't be able to listen to the message. When gestures *stop moving* they look more powerful.

◆ Your Voice

Your ability to vocalize means more than just speaking up so the audience can hear you. There are several elements of your vocal arrangement which can increase your effectiveness:

- ◆ Breathe between phrases
- ◆ Project to back of room
- ◆ Transition between visuals
- ◆ "Top-in" to emphasize
- ◆ Use the Rule of Three's
- ◆ When in doubt – pause first

◆ Proper Breathing

If you move around frequently when you present, you will eventually lose your breath from time to time. By breathing *between* phrases, rather then *during* phrases, you get the opportunity to vocalize better. If your words run together and you are speaking too quickly, your emphasis and inflection will be ineffective. By having enough air, you can say a longer phrase, more slowly, in order to make the audience understand more easily.

Try this. Take a deep breath. Did you expand your chest? Unfortunately, that is not the way we naturally breathe. The air normally goes into the lower abdomen.

You can test your normal breathing pattern by lying down on the floor, face up, with a book on your stomach. Breathe easily and notice the book moving up and down. Take a deep breath – it should be easy to make the book go up. Remove the book, stand up and take the same deep breath, but don't expand your chest or raise your shoulders. Your stomach should expand. That is the proper way to breathe when speaking.

Once you understand which muscles control breathing, you will be able to take in more air and sustain volume through the entire length of each phrase. Try this exercise. In one breath, say *"One by one, they went away."* Take another breath and add another number. Say, *"One by one, and two by two, they went away."* Take another breath and add another number as in, *"One by one, and two by two, and three by three, they went away."* With practice you should be able to sustain the phrase through the number *twelve.*

The key is having enough breath to complete long phrases or sentences without running out of air. Here is another exercise for breath control. It includes many "t" sounds which help with diction. If you pronounce every consonant your enunciation will improve. Moreover, you should be able to say this entire passage in one breath:

What a to do, to die today, at a minute or two to two
A thing distinctly hard to say, yet harder still to do
For they'll beat a tattoo at twenty to two
A rah-tah-tah–tah-tah-tah–tah-tah-tah–too
And the dragon will come at the sound of a drum
At a minute or two to two, today,
At a minute or two to two.

When you really develop excellent breath control, you should be able to say the above passage *two times* with one breath.

◆ Projecting Your Voice

People from all areas in the room must be able to hear *every* word you say. You must project your voice to the back of the room. The better your breath control, the easier this task will be. In addition, your awareness of projecting to the back of the room will keep your head up, facing forward as often as possible.

This doesn't mean you need to yell. It simply means that the intensity of your phrases, no matter how calm or soft-spoken, must always be audible.

When fielding responses from the audience, make sure you repeat the question or comment so the entire group can hear it. If you fail to do this, then your discussion will make sense only to those who heard the question or comment in the first place.

If you do turn your back to any section of the group for a moment, be sure to raise the volume of your voice so those behind you can still hear.

◆ Transitions

Have something to say *between* visuals, not just *during* visuals. This is less of a requirement when using slides or electronic images, since they change more rapidly. A more traditional medium, such as transparencies, requires personal attention to each visual.

The time it takes to remove one transparency from the overhead projector and replace it with the next can be several moments. Don't let that time be filled with *silence*. Have something to say as you approach the equipment, as you change the visual, as you set the next visual, and as you move away from the equipment.

It's not that you should talk constantly, but you should talk consistently to avoid large gaps of silence drawing attention to some activity.

Don't confuse silence with timed pauses. A timed pause lasts about three seconds and is useful to get the audience to think or to ponder a question. Dead silence tells the audience you couldn't really think of anything to say at the moment.

◆ "Topping-In"

When something is especially important on a visual or in your story, you can "top-in" with a phrase for emphasis. Simply, this means that your voice gets *louder* for the key word or phrase you are emphasizing.

Most of the time you will top-in when a new visual is displayed with a new heading or new topic. The *announcement* is done with more volume to attract attention.

◆ The Rule of Three's

Examine any political or religious speech. Key concepts or arguments are constructed around the Rule of Three's. For example, a politician may use the phrase: *"We will be more prosperous, we will pay less taxes, and our children will have a future."* Notice the use of *three references* to make a point.

People remember things in sets of three's. It's best to develop a vocal delivery which describes key points in groups of three's. Examine the difference between these phrases:

A good visual must be clear.

A good visual must be clear and concise.

A good visual must be clear, concise, and to the point.

The third phrase makes *three* references to the components of a "good" visual. Try to incorporate the Rule of Three's when building your next script for a presentation.

✦ Pause for a Moment

Have you ever been asked a question during your presentation and you didn't know the answer? There are two ways to approach the response. Incorrectly, would be to immediately look baffled, throw your hands up in the air and say *"Hey, I don't know!"* Correctly, would be to pause for a moment, as if you were *about* to answer the question, and then say *"Let me get back to you on that!"*

The pause maintains the level of credibility you held before the question was asked. The audience actually believes that you *could have answered* the question, given enough time. When in doubt, pause first. Don't stop there. Indicate that you intend to follow up at a later point.

✦ Vocal Problems

Avoid mumbling or speaking in low tones. Don't speak too quickly or your voice will sound garbled. Remember to adjust the pitch of your voice, now and then, to avoid a monotone sound. Make sure you maintain your volume throughout a phrase or your voice will drop off at the ends of sentences and be difficult to follow.

If you have an *accent*, as most of us do, it just means that you will sound different from what the audience may be used to hearing. If you have a well-rehearsed presentation and you can be understood when you speak, your accent will not reduce your effectiveness.

✦ Develop Your Own Style

In the long run, you need to be heard and seen while your visuals are displayed. Your appearance must be professional and your voice must be clear. Don't try to imitate other presenters, just be the best presenter you can be. Develop your own style and use the method of delivery which is most comfortable for you. There is no trick to this. You need to practice.

If you use the argument that you've been doing this for a number of years and you only need to WING it – then it will look like you WUNG it! Keep the following in mind each time you present:

The audience knows if you are less than prepared.

The audience knows if you are less than convinced.

The audience always knows.

Electronic Presentations

◆ Welcome to the Machine...

Throughout this book the concepts and ideas for developing more effective presentations apply to all current media formats that use color: overhead transparencies, 35mm slides, electronic visuals, etc. Invariably, you will experience a variety of formats depending on your particular business situation.

With the proliferation of personal computers, the ability to dictate the form and function of these media choices has reached the desktop and the technology that allows us to deliver "real-time" information is now within our grasp. We are talking about electronic presentations or electronic *screen shows* as they are so often described. As we become more and more *visual,* electronic support for content will be more the norm than the exception.

◆ Dealing with the Elements

Presentations are delivered away from the desktop, hence the issues of time and space come into play. The *time* it takes to reach a final result and/or make changes to that result and the *space* necessary to hold the visuals are important variables to consider.

With transparencies and 35mm slides, it takes time to create the output and time to make changes and re-create the output, once again. As the number of transparencies or slides increases, the physical space required to hold them also increases.

Electronic visuals more effectively handle the space and time issues by allowing multiple visuals to be contained in a small, single space (diskette), while offering instant access to the visuals for changes or updates to reflect more current information.

As the number of electronic visuals increases, only the amount of storage space for the visuals increases. With current technology, this can mean capacity for hundreds and hundreds of visuals without adding weight or volume to the equation.

◆ Building the Script

Since electronic presentations offer access to more information with more convenience regarding time and space, the manner in which you prepare your script should be different. You will have the ability to incorporate a greater number of visual "impressions" each containing more focused elements. Visuals with *less clutter* will facilitate understanding of key concepts.

What you once may have said with 11 overhead transparencies during a twenty-minute talk can be said with 35 electronic visuals over the same course of time. The opportunity lies in how you express the same information. Electronically you can change from one visual to the next more quickly, while incorporating techniques described earlier to reveal information in stages using builds and overlays.

A complicated visual may be treated in a variety of ways based simply on how you choose to present the image to the audience. Even the tools you use to create and display your visuals can impact the degree of flexibility available to you.

For example, suppose we have a map of the United States separated into three regions: West, East, and Central. Using a transparency, we may elect to display the map with each region noted in a different color. We would build a story to tell (script) around the single transparency. The visual would be displayed during the entire discussion of all three regions. Perhaps we would limit our discussion about each region so the transparency is not in view for an extended period. Notice that the *flexibility* in our script is somewhat limited by the media.

Using the same example of the map, the approach can be modified with electronic visuals. Using a sequence of *overlays*, the first image would show the entire map.

The next image would only change or brighten the color of one of the regions and a discussion of that region would begin. Since the visual looks the same, the *changed section* is considered an overlay.

The next image would dim the color of the first region and brighten or change the color of the next region to be discussed. This is the second overlay in our sequence. The last overlay would indicate that the third region is up for discussion as were the other two regions, before.

This series of *four impressions* using the same map allows the presenter to continue to hold attention through a series of changing images that are synchronized to an unfolding script. This reduces the amount of time a single visual impression is displayed and increases the effect of the script, overall. The total number of visuals has increased, but the communication process has been enhanced. Knowing this in advance gives us more flexibility with the script and allows us to consider additional possibilities, as well.

◆ Hyper-buttons

For the most part, presentations are strictly linear. One visual followed by the next and the next. This is most evident in 35mm slide presentations where the advance of the carousel dictates the order of the visuals. When we present in this *linear* fashion we preconceive our script to match the pattern. Once again, the flexibility of the script is somewhat limited by the media.

Electronic presentations offer a different element you may not have considered: the ability to present in a *non-linear* fashion. The opportunity to display, at any given moment, a visual which is out of sequence but well within the context of the script can be quite effective. Moreover, this nonlinear approach goes undetected by your audience since the random display still seems quite linear, as if the chosen visual were actually the next in sequence.

Let's use this technique with our prior example of the map which had three regions. Suppose during the discussion of the first region you had two additional visuals which added value to your discussion. Rather than displaying these visuals sequentially, you prefer to have the option of showing one or both of them at anytime during the presentation, only if you feel the need to use them. Let's call these additional images "back-up" visuals. Back-up visuals are useful to *add support* to your story when and if you need them.

Many presentation graphics software programs offer methods for *branching* or "jumping to" other visuals during an electronic presentation. You can create *action buttons* or *hyper-buttons* within a given visual which, when selected, may jump to any specified visual *within* the presentation, or launch a completely *separate* electronic presentation. The hyper-button may be visible or hidden and may take the form of a geometric shape or be part of an existing object, such as a single bar of a bar chart or even a specific region of a map, as in our example.

◆ Scripting Hyper-buttons

Continuing with our map example, suppose during our discussion of the first region we immediately decide that one of the back-up visuals needs to be referenced. If we designed our visual so that one of the states in the region functioned as a hyper-button, then during the presentation we only need select (or click with a remote mouse) the area of the hyper-button in order to jump to the back-up visual associated with the button.

The process would appear to be sequential to the audience, but the actual location of the back-up visual might be at the very end (after the last image) in the presentation. Best of all, the choice to use the hyper-button is now conditional of circumstances happening at the moment.

The use of hyper-buttons for nonlinear activity goes beyond back-up visuals. You may use hyper-buttons to launch completely different software *applications* or play *multimedia* objects such as sound, animation or full-motion video.

Imagine our map split into three regions, each region supported by back-up visuals, each back-up visual capable of launching a detailed spreadsheet further supporting the data on the back-up visual. This ability to "drill down" to fine detail opens up numerous possibilities for on-the-spot access to critical information.

Hyper-buttons offer you the opportunity to plan a series of alternatives in anticipation of questions, in deference to time constraints, or relative to other activities so often associated with group dynamics.

Electronic visuals allow you to approach your story with more creativity than the approach you might take with other media formats. The flexibility to create very conceptual visuals supported by instant access to detailed information changes the way you develop the script.

◆ Continuity

A major advantage to electronic presentations is the seamless transition from one visual to the next. Unlike other media formats, the flow of electronic information is virtually uninterrupted as the story unfolds for the audience. Even if the script incorporates action or hyper-buttons for branching, the *transition effects* (electronic changes from one visual to the next) allow the presenter to maintain a continuity which increases the overall attention span of the audience. Accessing a back-up visual is exactly the same as advancing to any other visual in sequence. The underlying issue is one of *continuity*.

At MediaNet, our studies have shown that periodic breaks in the flow of the presentation become more distracting as time continues. For example, the physical move required to change a transparency disrupts the presentation simply because the action is not associated with the delivery of information. A solution might be to have an assistant change the transparency while the presenter maintains a steady position from which to speak.

Of course, the continuity will still be broken by the removal of one transparency and placement of the next. Most times this results in a reflection of white light from the overhead projector. Even turning the projector off between changes and turning the projector on for the next transparency still causes the interruption of information. 35mm slides have a similar problem with continuity, but the transition from one slide to the next is much faster and the distraction is less noticeable than with transparencies.

Electronic visuals, by maintaining continuity, allow the audience to scan each image more quickly with less distraction. Once the visual information is noted, the audience has time to focus on the presenter and listen to what is being verbalized. The more time for the audience to listen, the more effective the presenter will be.

◆ Weighing the Options

We touched on *portability* earlier, but the issue needs to be considered in light of the equipment necessary to effectively deliver electronic presentations. Currently, any presentation you give involves carrying your visuals in some form or another. Whether you have a tray of slides, a folder of transparencies, or a diskette with electronically stored visuals, additional equipment is always required.

You typically need a slide projector for the slides, an overhead projector for the transparencies, a computer and a projection device for the electronic visuals, etc. If the issue is weight, it would appear the combination of a portable computer and portable projection device would be much heavier than the other alternatives.

The type of projection device for the electronic presentation, however, may not require a computer at all. Some projection devices have a built-in storage device to allow the presenter to eliminate the need to carry a computer in order to present electronically.

Many projectors are built with a smaller *footprint* and some are the size and *weight* of the notebook computer used to deliver the presentation. This increase in the portability of these devices allows a presenter to travel with the complete package — the data source (computer) and the light source (projector).

When you can have control over the external elements (equipment) associated with your presentation, you will have less technical surprises waiting for you when you arrive at the location of your event.

◆ A Room with a View

When presenting electronically you need to consider other elements specifically related to the location of the event. Items such as the room lighting, the projector brightness, the type of projection screen, and the manner in which you handle the technology, all come into play during an electronic presentation.

Understanding room layout issues will help you better plan each event. You can also visit MediaNet's web site (www.medianet-ny.com) for more information on room set-up, seating and other logistics.

✦ Lighting

The goal is to attain an *unequal distribution* of light. The best lighting environment casts no light on the projection screen, some light over the audience and a great deal of light on the presenter. In the absence of stage lighting, a slide projector and/or overhead projector can be used to fill the presentation area with more light than the given light in the room.

Avoid fluorescent lighting, since it is designed to cast light across a very broad area and it will easily wash out the image on your screen. *Incandescent lighting* works best since you can usually control the brightness with dimmer switches. In some situations you may need to remove one or more incandescent lights in the front of the room to reduce the amount of light on the screen, while leaving the remaining lights bright enough for the audience to take notes.

If you are working with a spot light, make sure you can handle the bright light without excessively blinking or squinting. If you are able to position spot lights, use two of them, on opposite sides of the room, and aim them at you to cover both your *rest* and *power* positions. This is also known as *cross-lighting*.

✦ Image

Projector brightness is critical for electronic presentations, especially where control of the room lighting is difficult. With electronic projectors, we recommend the projector be at least 450 *lumens*. Lumens are simply a measure of light intensity. The higher the lumens, the brighter the light and the result is a more visually pleasing image when projected. Regarding resolution (such as SVGA, XGA, etc.) try to use a projector with a maximum resolution *greater* than that of your computer. This lets you keep your computer display visible as you present. Using the computer like a small "prompter", you'll spend less time glancing back to look at the projected image and more time facing the audience.

✦ Screen

The most versatile projection screens are those that allow for the best viewing from all angles. We recommend a flat, non-glare, matte white screen. In addition, the screen should be *keystone correcting*.

Keystoning is a problem that occurs when the projecting device is positioned lower than the projection screen. The greater the angle the more the visual appears like the letter "V", wider at the top and thinner at the bottom.

A keystone correcting screen has an extension bar at the top. When the bar is extended, the screen is able to hook onto the bar at any of several tabs or notches depending on how far forward you wish the screen to lean. The more you tilt the screen toward the projector the more the image becomes square. The keystone correcting feature is usually found on most screens with heights of 7 feet or less.

If the ceiling height allows, make sure the *bottom* of the screen is above your shoulders as you stand at floor level. This will make it easier for everyone to see more of the visual from any point in the room.

◆ Technology

Don't get surprised by the technology. For example, if you are using a notebook computer with an electronic projector, make sure you are somewhat familiar with the equipment. You may have to arrive a few minutes early to make sure the technology will function properly.

If you encounter technical problems during the presentation, don't try to hide those problems from the audience. Immediately announce any problem and offer an estimate of how long it might take to resolve the difficulty. If you suspect it will take longer than five minutes to resolve, suggest a break. If a break is not feasible at that moment, ask the audience if they (as a group) will allow you to take a few moments to rectify the problem.

Should they object to the delay or if you anticipate a long delay you may have to end the presentation. In all cases, explain any problems. You may actually find members of the audience who have experienced similar situations and who may offer solutions, right on the spot.

Make sure you hide the wires. The awkward appearance of several cables and power cords, dangling in front of the audience, will be a distraction. A cluttered look indicates a less than polished presentation. In addition, make sure power cords or other wires are taped down or secured to avoid someone accidentally tripping over them.

Finally, have a back-up plan, just in case. Depending on the complexity of your presentation, a diskette containing a copy of your visuals may be enough. Of course, if your computerized device is not operating you may need to consider alternative media such as 35mm slides or color overhead transparencies. Whatever it takes to allow you to continue with the presentation is the back-up you need, unless you prefer to handle the consequences of not giving the presentation at that time. When all else fails, always be prepared to reschedule the event!

Conclusion

This book is not the final word on presentations. It is simply a strategy which has proven to be successful. The principles of Purpose, Movement and Color are inherent to the natural process of human behavior. At MediaNet, we firmly believe that the one thing that remains constant is people. A presenter looks for *similarities* among the audience members, rather than differences. They may appear unique, but when building effective visuals, the appeal must be to *common traits* among all people. Can they *see* the screen? Can they *understand* the information? Can they *remember* the main concepts presented?

So often we have seen presentations tailored to job-specific groups rather than to groups of people with jobs. For example, the tendency is to categorize people by what they do for a living, such as *accounting types* or *engineering types*. There are only two types of people, *living* and *dead*. You decide which type you're presenting to and strategize from there.

The premise to work from is that people are generally about the same. Granted, we all have our unique ways, but we are first and foremost *human*. If you approach every audience from this initial point, you can develop clear, *conceptual* presentations. Naturally, more *technical* presentations demand an audience with a higher level of *expertise* in a given subject matter, but this should not change the approach to the *design* of the visuals. Just because some people are technically proficient doesn't mean they suddenly prefer charts cluttered with information! Knowledge doesn't change the way people *see*.

If you follow our advice and stay focused on your objective, examine each visual as to how the audience will look at the image, and remain consistent with your color choices, you will have a more effective presentation.

It's all about *change*. By **changing** the way the audience *thinks*, the way the audience *sees*, and the way the audience *feels*, you will have a presentation that is more ***effective***.

It's about **Purpose, Movement, and Color**. It's a *strategy* for effective presentations.

...And it works!

Looking Ahead...

The dawn of the information age indicates a variety of media choices for delivering information. 35mm slides and color transparencies are still useful formats, but the advent of personal computers and advanced projection display technology has allowed electronic presentations to become a much more versatile and highly flexible format.

The unique elements of electronic presentations include other segments, as well. The ability to incorporate sound, video, and animation into a multimedia electronic presentation adds to both the flexibility and the complexity of the event. Technologically, it keeps getting easier and easier to add a variety of media choices to the presentation. Yet, these options add to the time it takes to gather, sort, edit, choose and effectively merge a variety of media into a presentable format. The *production* aspects always need to be considered.

When dealing with multimedia elements you have to consider a number of critical issues. For example, what effect does moving footage with voice narration have on the presenter? Which element, sound or video, commands the most attention? What control is lost during an interactive presentation with a large group? Can we mix multiple media formats and maintain continuity? Are we facing multimedia or *multi-mania*?

As the world becomes more and more visual, the role of presentations will change to reflect the power of electronic communication. The growing influence of the World Wide Web over the way we do business is changing constantly. Information is exchanged over internet, intranet and extranet web sites; meetings take place through webcasting, videoconferencing, and desktop conferencing; interactive television and virtual reality will allow presentations to conquer the limits of time and distance.

These and other issues force us to constantly change the way we approach new concepts, new markets, and new technologies.

**A new world of presentations
is always beginning!**

More About MediaNet...

◆ Seminars & Workshops

MediaNet offers a number of different lectures that can be grouped together into an *Electrifying Presentations* event. Typically, one of these presentation skills workshops consists of a combination of lectures and a few individual coaching sessions. Organizations can have a skills workshop tailored to fit the needs of the particular group.

For high-level skill development, MediaNet has a special *Presentation Skills Mastery Program* offered by invitation only. This intensive, long-term skills program is designed only for those who truly wish to *master* the skill of presenting to the highest level possible.

◆ Creative Services

MediaNet designs presentations in all media formats. *Creative services* range from initial consultation on the script to the final production of slides, transparencies, electronic visuals, multimedia events, and more. We apply the principles discussed in this book to each presentation we develop.

◆ Publications & Software

The Art of Presenting™ is a CD-ROM that contains over six hours of *interactive* content. Several virtual reality lectures explain content development, visual design and delivery skills through an entertaining combination of video, audio, animation and graphics.

MediaNet has compiled its extensive research into a software expert system called **ShowSTARTER**®. Like a *consultant-on-disk*, this unique program uses artificial intelligence to build a complete presentation strategy based on responses to a simple 10-question survey.

MediaNet's *Electrifying Templates*™ series offer a variety of layout themes. Simply incorporate one of the templates into the visual design layout of your presentation to assure a consistency in your message.

Tom Mucciolo is co-author of another book, *Special Edition Using Microsoft PowerPoint 2000* (1999, Macmillan Computer Publishing), which combines the study of a software program with the complete skills associated with presenting.

For the most up-to-date information, visit us on the web at
www.medianet-ny.com